Diana Lawrenson

PICTURES BY Geoff Kelly

IT'S TRUE!

YOUR BONES ARE
STRONGER THAN
CONCRETE

ALLEN&UNWIN

First published in 2007

Allen & Unwin
83 Alexander Street
Crows Nest NSW 2065
Australia
Phone: (61 2) 8425 0100
Fax: (61 2) 9906 2218
Email: info@allenandunwin.com
Web: www.allenandunwin.com

National Library of Australia
Cataloguing-in-Publication entry:

Lawrenson, Diana.
It's true! your bones are stronger than concrete.
Bibliography.
Includes index.
ISBN 978 1 74114 732 2.
1. Bones. I. Kelly, Geoff. II. Title. (Series: It's true; 26)
611.71

Series, cover and text design by Ruth Grüner
Cover photographs: Spike Mafford/Getty Images (skeleton)
and Nicholas Monu/istockphoto.com (bones)
Set in 12.5pt Minion by Ruth Grüner
Printed by McPherson's Printing Group

1 3 5 7 9 10 8 6 4 2

**Teaching notes for the It's True! series are available
on the website: www.itstrue.com.au**

Contents

WHY BONES?

At school I envied people with broken limbs in plaster casts that everyone signed. Then I saw a girl after she'd been thrown from a motor bike. Her jagged, bloodied thighbone was sticking out of her leg, and after that I changed my mind.

Without bones we'd be nothing but a skin bag full of guts, flopped on the floor. Candles, soap, fertilisers, Gran's best teacups and jelly are made from ground-up bones. Bones are used for decorating walls and noses. If you want to find out about skulls and skeletons, weaver's bottom, how bones rot, or how the pirate flag got its name, all you have to do is dip into this book. You'll also find out what happened to Santa Claus's nose and what bones have to do with mystery, history and science.

Diana Lawrenson

1

Who was it?

Imagine hiking through the bush, or scuffing your feet along a dry riverbed, or exploring a cave. You trip on a skull . . . or a whole human skeleton. Who might these bones belong to? A murder victim, someone who got lost bushwalking, or a skeleton from ancient times?

If you contact the police, they'll call in forensic scientists to examine these bones.

Using microscopes and chemical tests, the scientists will find out:

>> how long ago the person died
>> whether it was a man or a woman
>> roughly how old the person was
>> what race they belonged to

» how tall they were, and

» how they died.

MAN OR WOMAN?

To decide the sex of the body, scientists look at the pelvis and the skull. The pelvis is a girdle of bones that looks a bit like a basin with a large hole in it. Our hips are part of the pelvis.

A male pelvis and a female pelvis are different shapes. A female pelvis is shallow, and wide enough for a baby to pass through during birth. A male pelvis is narrower and deeper. During childbirth some scarring occurs on part of the mother's pelvis, so a forensic scientist can tell from a woman's bones whether or not she has had a baby.

Male skulls tend to be bigger than female ones, and the male jaw is heavier.

And just to make really sure, the scientists will check for the Y chromosome – the chromosome that men have in all their body cells and women don't.

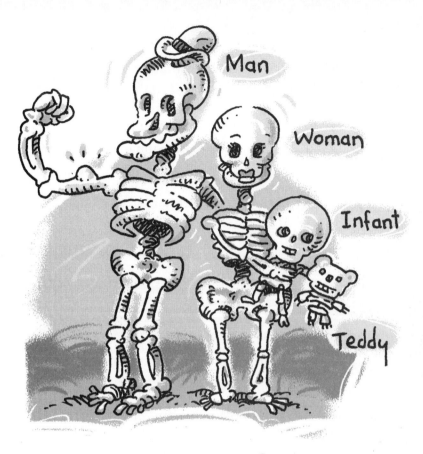

Man

Woman

Infant

Teddy

YOUNG OR OLD?

At birth each part of the skeleton is perfectly formed.
These shapes are made of cartilage, which is a whitish,
bendy substance like a jelly-snake. As babies and
children grow, more and more calcium is deposited
in the cartilage and it ossifies – hardens into bone.

Eventually some bones fuse together. For example, the two sides of your mandible (jawbone) fused to become the single bone of your chin when you were about two years old. The humerus – the bone in your upper arm – is in three bony parts during childhood. It grows in length from cartilage growth plates near its upper and lower ends. These growth plates close at around 14 years, leaving you with one long bone – not three!

In the same way, your thigh bones each consist of three bony parts separated by growth cartilages, but by around 18 years these will have fused and you will have a large single bone, the femur, in each upper leg.

The bones of your pelvis fuse after puberty.

Forensic scientists know the approximate ages the growth plates of different bones close. They also know how diseases such as arthritis and osteoporosis affect bones, mostly in older people. All this helps towards working out the age of the person the skeleton belonged to, but age can't be told accurately from bones alone.

STRUGGLE AND STRANGULATION

Once flesh has disappeared, the state of the bones may be the only clue to the cause of death. If skull bones are cracked or dinted, the dead person might have received a heavy blow to the head. Or they might have fallen or been pushed onto rocks. Ribs might show cut marks that are evidence of stab wounds, or they may reveal bullet damage. The shape of the marks can suggest the type of gun or knife used for murder.

There's also a bone that might show if a person was strangled. The hyoid bone is a U-shaped, fragile bone in the throat. You can't feel it, but without it you couldn't speak because it's an essential part of your voicebox. It sits beneath your tongue and above your Adam's apple – the lumpy bit at the front of your throat. In quite a lot of strangulations the hyoid bone is fractured.

WHICH HAND?

Bones will show if a person was right- or left-handed. The joint socket in the shoulder blade of whichever arm the person wrote with will be more worn than the socket on the other side.

THE BEST TEST

DNA, deoxyribonucleic acid, can remain in the cells of human bones for about 30 years after death. If it can be matched with DNA from another part of that person (e.g. a yanked-out hair on a hairbrush), it helps prove identity. But what if nothing like that is available?

Inside all our cells are mitochondria that generate energy. Mitochondria have their own DNA (mtDNA) which is inherited by boys and girls only from their mothers. It is different from DNA in the nucleus of our cells. If the mtDNA in bones can be matched to the mtDNA of a relative through the maternal line, it can help establish whose these bones are.

DNA can be destroyed in skeletons ravaged by bushfires.

REBUILDING FACES

Can you find out what a skull's face was like before the flesh rotted away?

Yes, scientists can construct one quite like it. They know how thick our flesh is in different places – for example, on our foreheads, on our chins.

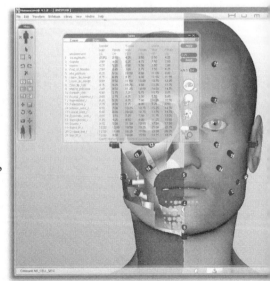

Experts can draw a three-dimensional (3D) face on a computer and apply virtual muscles and skin. Or they can make a model of the head and apply plasticine or modelling clay to the right depth at different places. Noses are tricky because they are mostly not bone, so the nose shape can only be guessed.

The reconstruction might then be matched with a 'missing person' photo to help determine who the skull belonged to.

THE FACE OF SANTA CLAUS

People have used fossilised skulls to reconstruct the faces of early humans. They've even done it for Father Christmas!

The bones of Saint Nicholas, the saint on whom Santa Claus is based, are in the crypt of a church in Bari, Italy.

A British expert, Caroline Wilkinson, used skull measurements and X-rays in 2004 to reconstruct the Saint's face. His bones show he was a heavy-set man, rather like a rugby player. We think of him as kind and cheerful, but there's a story he punched a bishop. Forensic experts found Saint Nick had a broken nose – maybe the bishop punched back!

2

Skulls and crossbones

How would you have felt if you were on a sailing ship in the 1700s, being chased by another boat flying a skull and crossbones flag? Dead scared, most likely.

That was exactly what the Jolly Roger – the skull and crossbones flag – was meant to do: scare people. It wasn't jolly. The more afraid a boat's crew and passengers were, the more likely they were to hand over their valuables and the ship's cargo to pirates.

PIRATES' PERSONALS

English, French and Spanish pirates used the Jolly Roger. Some pirates had their own flag design. Edward

Teach, called Blackbeard, flew one showing a skeleton with devil-like horns on a black background. The skeleton held an hourglass in one hand, and in the other an arrow piercing a heart that dripped blood. The flag of Jack Rackham (Calico Jack) was a skull above two crossed cutlasses. Christopher Condent's had a row of three skulls above crossbones.

One of the cheekiest flags belonged to Bartholomew Roberts, better known as Black Bart. On it a clothed seafarer held either a drink (or perhaps it's an hourglass) jointly with a skeleton.

The skull and bones represented death, knives and cutlasses symbolised violence, and hourglasses indicated time. Wings on an hourglass emphasised that time was running out fast for the boat being chased.

THE BLOODY FLAG

The Jolly Roger wasn't the flag mariners feared most. The worst was the pirates' plain red one, the bloody flag. The red flag meant 'No quarter given' ('No mercy will be shown'). In other words, the decks would be

awash with blood and you'd be lucky to escape alive if
your ship was caught.

The name Jolly Roger may have come from the red
flag. French pirates called it *la jolie rouge*, meaning
'pretty red'. Perhaps English pirates pronounced this
as 'jolly roger'. Or it could have come from 'Old Roger',
once a nickname for the Devil. Then there was a pirate
who terrorised vessels in the Indian Ocean. His name,
Ali Raja, may have been distorted to Jolly Roger.

Yes, Cut-throat, I agree it is a very Jolly Roger but I think you are missing the point!

CROSS YOUR LEGS

In Scottish churchyards
skulls and crossbones
are carved on some
tombstones. They date back to the 1300s, the time of
the Knights Templar, an order of French knights.

When the king of France executed many of the
knights and confiscated their wealth, some of the
survivors fled to Scotland. The skull and crossbones
was the emblem of these knights, and when they died
their leg bones were removed and placed in the shape
of a cross at burial.

HALLOWEEN

Celebrations on 31 October go back almost 2000 years.
For Celtic people it was Samhain, the day between the
end of summer and the beginning of the cold, dark
winter – and the day spirits of the dead roamed about.
People dressed up in frightening costumes and lit fires
to keep any evil spirits away.

A few hundred years later Samhain became a Christian festival, All-Hallows Eve. This was the day before All Souls' Day on 1 November. Eventually All Hallows Eve became known as Hallowe'en (*e'en* means even, eve or evening), and skulls and skeletons became part of the costumes that people dressed up in.

GRIM AND GRISLY

Have you seen pictures of the Grim Reaper – a skeleton wearing a black hood and gown and carrying a scythe? That scythe isn't for slashing grass or wheat. The Grim Reaper is Death, mowing down people, mowing down life. Scary.

DEAD END

What happens to the body when someone dies?

A body in the open can rot away to a skeleton very quickly in hot, moist conditions and with the help of birds, insects, fungi and bacteria. Sometimes this happens in only a few weeks. If wild animals or rodents have been foraging, the bones may be chewed and widely scattered. Bones will dissolve in very acid soil, which is why you don't see piles of them in tropical forests even though lots of animals live there.

Buried bodies take longer to rot, especially if they are in a box or a coffin. The bones will become dry after about 40 years and then may last thousands of years if they become mineralised (see Chapter 8).

Bodies that are dried by wind and heat in deserts, or freeze-dried in ice, can last for thousands of years because bacteria and other microbes can't act on dried-out flesh. Think of Egyptian mummies, and Ötzi, the Neolithic 'Ice Man' who lay frozen for more than 5000 years in the European Alps.

GOODBYE

When someone dies we have to decide what to do with the body.

Chinese people traditionally bury their dead on a hillside. The Japanese, who are mainly Buddhist, mostly cremate (burn) theirs. Hindus in India and Bali burn their loved ones on a funeral pyre in the open. Muslims choose burial. Some Australian Aborigines would leave a body in a tree or a narrow opening between rocks or a cave; others might cremate or bury their dead.

The Parsees of Mumbai in India have always left their dead at the stone Towers of Silence for vultures to pick the bones clean. But now most of the vultures in south-east Asia have disappeared. Why? They ate

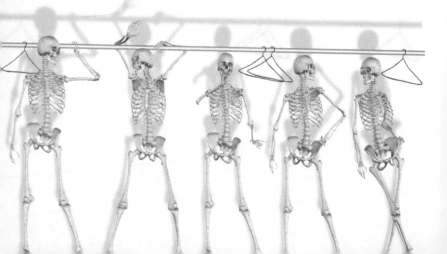

the carcasses of cattle treated with a medicine that was lethal to the birds. Now some Parsees want to breed vultures and keep them in cages at the Towers.

In Western countries people are buried in cemeteries or cremated (out of sight and after a service) in a special oven at a funeral parlour. The flesh and bones turn to ash. The ash can be buried at the foot of a shrub in a memorial garden, or put in a wall cavity with a plaque showing the dead person's name. Sometimes the ash is returned to the relatives so they can scatter it somewhere meaningful – such as the sea if the person enjoyed sailing.

DECORATING WITH DEATH

Cemeteries in Paris became really overcrowded in the late 1700s. Between three and six *million* skeletons were moved from crowded churchyards to old Roman tunnels and limestone quarries beneath the city. If you ever go to Paris, spook yourself by taking a tour of the Catacombs. Thousands of skulls and bones are piled in amazing patterns along corridors.

The Czech town of Sedlec has an ossuary – a place where bones are kept – in its chapel. The bones date back to the 1300s, when a disease known as 'the Black Death' killed nearly half the population of Europe. Other bones are from wars in the 1400s. In 1870 a woodcarver, Frantisek Rint, used about 40 000 of Sedlec's skeletons to decorate the ossuary. Guess what he hung from the ceiling? A chandelier he'd made with every bone in the human body.

In Rome you can visit the crypt beneath the church of Santa Maria della Concezione. Here you'll see chapel walls decorated with the bones of thousands of former Capuchin monks. The Italian inscription translates as:

'We were what you are, and what we are you will be.'

OCEAN GRAVES

Plenty of shipwrecks lie on the ocean floor, still holding their treasure of gold and porcelain and pottery. Why don't divers find skeletons there too? What happened to the bones of the crews and passengers after fish ate the flesh?

Sea isopods are small crab-like creatures that *love* bone and bone marrow. If a body comes their way, they zero in for a feast. Minerals in salt water speed up the rotting process, and eventually nothing is left.

THE DAYS OF THE DEAD

Mexicans celebrate the lives of their dead relations at the time of Halloween, All Souls' Day and All Saints'

Day – 31 October and 1 and 2 November. They have picnics beside graves in cemeteries, and some will reverently clean the bones of their family members.

Bakers bake tiny loaves of bread and top them with crust 'bones', while chocolate skulls and skeletons are yummy treats.

Death isn't frightening, the Mexicans say, but the living sometimes are.

3

Various vertebrates

Bend over and feel the line of knobbly
bits that makes up your backbone. Each
knob is part of a vertebra. Animals that
have backbones – like us – are called
vertebrates. Mammals, birds, reptiles,
amphibians and fish are vertebrates.[1]

[1] Insects, worms, jellyfish and some sea
creatures are **in**vertebrates – they don't
have a backbone. A few make up for it
by having an exoskeleton (an external
or outside skeleton). Think of crabs,
or beetles. Exoskeletons are not made
of bone.

Today the largest and smallest vertebrates live in the sea. The stout infantfish is less than 9 millimetres long, while the blue whale can reach almost 30 metres.

All vertebrates have skulls, jaws, backbones and ribs. Some also have limb bones, and others have wing, fin or flipper bones.

FINNY BUSINESS

Fish skeletons are made of bone or cartilage.

Fish with bony skeletons, such as salmon, goldfish and piranhas, have swim bladders that can fill with various gases, a bit like a hot-air balloon. This helps them rise through the water when they need to. When they want to dive deeper they expel the gas.

Sharks and their relatives, rays, don't have swim bladders. Their skeletons are made of cartilage which is lighter and much more flexible than bone – picture a ray 'flapping' gracefully through the water. Sharks and rays also have extremely large, oily livers. Because the oil is lighter than water, it helps them 'float'. Some sharks gulp air, too, which increases their buoyancy.

The 'swords' of the marlin and swordfish are actually long upper jaws that they use as a weapon when hunting seafood. The invertebrate octopus has to scoot for cover . . .

BEETLE CLEAN-UP

Museums of natural history keep colonies of Dermestid beetles. What for? They crawl through all the nooks and crannies of dead creatures, eating every bit of flesh until the only things left are . . . bones for display.

Professor . . . the Dermestid beetles have escaped!

FLY? YOU WISH

Next time you finish eating the meat from a chicken leg, take the bone outside and break it open. Instead of solid bone you'll see lots of tiny air spaces. This makes the bone very light, which helps when a bird wants to fly.

Pulling the wishbone is an old custom. After a meal of roast chicken, you leave the breastbone aside to dry. Later, you and someone else hook your little fingers around each prong of the bone and pull until it breaks. The person who ends up with the bigger bit can then make a wish.

SSSSSWIM LIKE AN S

The backbones of reptiles are much more flexible than bird and mammal backbones because of the way their vertebrae are linked together.

Watch a snake swim like an S, or rear up suddenly to bite you, thanks to its backbone joints and muscles. Snakes have from 160 to 400 pairs of ribs attached to their vertebrae, depending on the species. We humans have only 12.

HORNY HEADGEAR

Antlers are branching, bony growths that some mammals such as deer have. The antlers are covered with skin and hair called velvet. Velvet is highly prized in Asia as a health tonic. Each year the animals shed their antlers and then begin growing new ones.

Horns can be straight or curled, but they are never branched like antlers. They have a bony core that's covered with keratin – the substance our fingernails are made of.

The Downside of Antlers

During the mating season, animals with horns and antlers use them to fight over females.

Animals such as cattle and rams don't shed their horns the way deer shed their antlers. But the horns used to be cut off and used as drinking horns, trumpets and even containers for gunpowder.

Rhinoceros horns are not true horns because they consist of a hair-like substance and don't grow from a bony base.

TEETH AND TUSKS

Teeth are *not* bones, even though you often see them in a skull. They are made of dentine and enamel, which is not what bones are made of. Animals' tusks are enlarged teeth.

4

A squiz at skeletons

In the 1500s a judge gave the Flemish anatomist, Andreus Vesalius, corpses from the gallows (bodies from people who'd been hanged). Why? So Vesalius could dissect them. Vesalius wrote a book which greatly expanded our understanding of the human body.

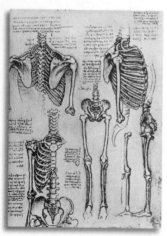

Leonardo da Vinci, the famous Italian artist and inventor, was given permission to dissect bodies at Italian hospitals. His magnificent paintings and sculptures reveal his knowledge of anatomy, although *his* book of pictures of the body wasn't published until 1680, well over a century after his death.

BODY-SNATCHING – A GRAVE CRIME

For a long time in the United Kingdom the only bodies anatomists could lawfully use were those of criminals who had been sentenced first to hang, then to be dissected after death – an extra punishment.

When anatomy schools couldn't obtain enough bodies, criminals began stealing freshly buried ones from graves. Surgeons bought these bodies for dissection demonstrations. Some people were murdered to supply them, too.

The Bodysnatcher and the Head Hunter flip for the body

At the Glasnevin Cemetery in Ireland, body-snatching became such a problem that watchtowers were built to keep a lookout for the robbers. Night-watchmen and hounds were employed, but it was difficult for the dogs to tell the difference between the nightwatchmen, visitors and body-snatchers . . . so the dogs had to go.

The Anatomy Act was a law passed in Britain in 1832 to stop the grave-robbing, and to permit people to donate their bodies. It also allowed unclaimed bodies from the poorhouse to be used for medical demonstrations.

MODEL BONES

Like our skin and other organs, our bones are constantly producing new cells as old ones die off. This process is called remodelling.

When you reach your full height at around 18, people say you've 'stopped growing', but you'll only have stopped growing *taller*. Remodelling continues.

FRAMED

Bones are our frame that keeps us upright. Many also protect soft and vital parts of our body from harm. Your skull protects your brain. Your ribcage protects your heart and lungs. Your vertebrae protect your spinal cord – the soft rope of nerves that links every part of the body to the brain.

TWO IN ONE

We have two skeletons that are joined to each other.

The **axial** skeleton – the **axis** of the body – is made up of our backbone, skull and ribcage.

Our **appendicular** skeleton includes the bones of our **appendages** – our limbs.

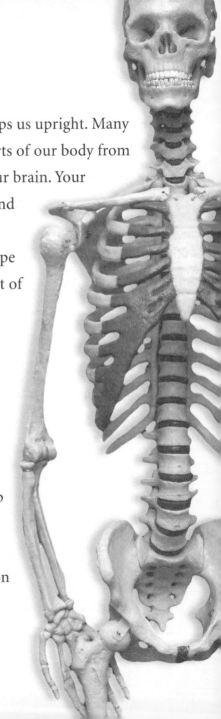

GIRDLES FOR GUYS AND GIRLS

Our limbs fit into two girdles.

Our shoulderblades and collarbones form our **pectoral girdle** that is attached to the sternum (breastbone). It lets us make lots of upper-arm movements with the help of muscles that are attached to each scapula (shoulder blade).

The **pelvic girdle** is much stronger. It protects some of the body's intestines, and also supports some of the body weight above it. The pelvis is made up of three fused bones on each side: the ilium (ill-ee-um) which your hips are part of, the ischium (ish-ee-um) which is the bone you sit on, and the pubis (pew-bis) at the front, below your belly button. At the back the pelvis is attached to the sacrum, which is part of your spine. Your upper leg bones fit into the pelvis.

TOUGH NUT

The cranium is made up of eight bones that form the forehead and the rounded parts at the top, sides and back of our head. Of the 14 bones in our face, only one can move. It's the jawbone. (The one that's moving when your teacher says, 'Who's talking?') The nose consists of two short bones – plus some cartilage, the part you can twitch.

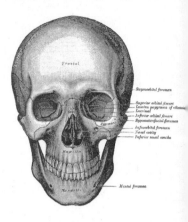

Can you work out how many bones are in a skull?

OVER AND OUT

As a baby is being born, its cranial bones slide over each other. This makes the skull small enough to fit through the mother's birth canal.

Have you ever felt the 'soft spot' on the top of a baby's head? It's the fontanelle, which means 'little fountain', and it pulsates – like a little throbbing fountain. The bones of the cranium don't quite meet here, and the space is covered by tough membrane and skin. There's another of these soft spots at the back. The fontanelles give a baby's brain room when it's growing fast in the first 18 months after birth.

Yes, he takes after his father...they both have holes in their heads

The fontanelle at the back closes when the baby is about 6 weeks old. The one at the top closes about 18 months later.

LISTEN 'ERE!

Did you know you had bones inside your ears? These are the ossicles – three tiny bones named for their strange shapes: the malleus (hammer), the incus (anvil) and the stapes (stirrup). They transmit waves of sound from the eardrum through to the brain. They are **not** counted as bones of the skull.

The stapes is the smallest bone in the body and is about the size of a grain of rice.

Our outer, fleshy ears are made of cartilage, not bone. That's why you won't find ears on a skeleton.

A IS FOR ATLAS, V IS FOR VERTEBRAE

Our skull sits on our cervical (neck) vertebrae. The first, the top one, is called atlas. It's named after Atlas, the giant in Greek mythology who carried the skies on his shoulders. The axis is the second cervical vertebra. It has a bony peg that fits into the atlas, and together they allow us to nod and shake our heads.

Doctors use less interesting names. They call these two vertebrae C1 and C2 – short for Cervical 1, Cervical 2. The other five cervical vertebrae are (surprise) C3, C4, C5, C6 and C7. These are the knobbly bits you can feel at the back of your neck.

All the other vertebrae are numbered in groups in a similar way, so altogether we have:

» 7 cervical vertebrae, C1 to C7, in the neck

» 12 thoracic vertebrae, T1 to T12, in the chest, with a pair of ribs attached to each

- 5 lumbar vertebrae, L1 to L5, forming the lower back and supporting a lot of the body's weight
- 5 sacral vertebrae fused together (in adults) to form the sacrum – a large, strong, triangular bone attached to, and wedged between, the pelvis. The sacral bones are not numbered because they are fused
- 4 small vertebrae fused together (in adults) to form the coccyx (kok-six) – the tailbone. It's called the coccyx because it's curved and looks like a cuckoo's beak (*kokkus* is Greek for cuckoo).

WAGGING IT

We can't wag our tails like dogs or switch them like horses because we don't have enough tailbones. Lots of animals have a coccyx with more vertebrae than us (a horse has 15–20). These vertebrae stay separate, unlike ours, so with the help of muscles they can swing into action.

TRUE, FALSE OR FLOATING

We have twelve pairs of ribs, and each pair is attached at the back to a thoracic vertebra. The first seven pairs, the **true ribs**, are also attached in the front to the sternum – the breastbone.

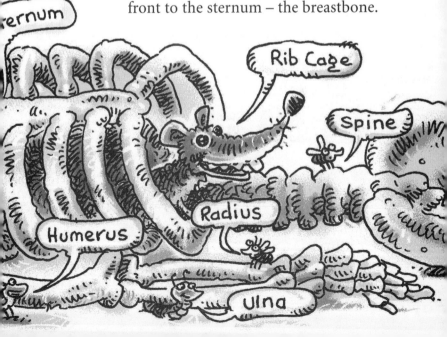

The next three pairs, called **false ribs**, are attached to the sternum via the cartilage of the seventh rib. The two pairs at the bottom aren't attached to the sternum at all and so are called **floating ribs**.

LIMBERING UP PLUS PLUS

In each leg, heel and ankle we have:

» femur + patella + tibia + fibula + 7 tarsals.

In each foot we have:

» 5 metatarsals + 14 phalanges (2 in the big toe, 3 in each of the other toes).

In each arm and wrist we have:

» humerus + radius + ulna + 8 carpals.

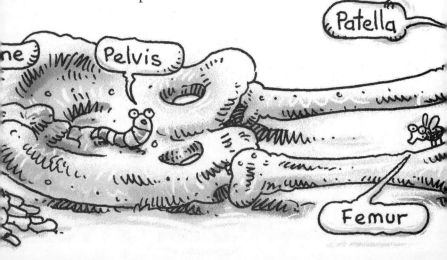

In each hand we have:

» 5 metacarpals + 14 phalanges (2 in the thumb, 3 in each of the other fingers).

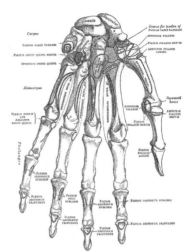

NUMBER-CRUNCHING

Have you been counting the limb bones? What's the total? (Remember to double for the second arm and leg.)

Now add on the vertebrae (the sacrum and the coccyx count only as one each because they're fused), the 8 cranial (skull) bones, the 14 facial bones, the ossicles (remember each ear),

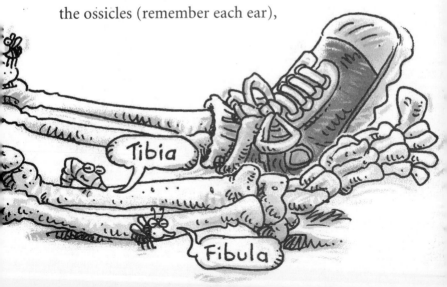

Tibia

Fibula

the hyoid bone in the throat, both sides of the pectoral (shoulder) girdle, the sternum (breastbone), the ribs (don't forget they're pairs), the bones from the pelvic girdle (they're fused, so count only one for each side), and you get . . . what?

PUN THAT'S NOT FUN

At the inner side of the bony part of the elbow, a knob of the humerus sticks out just where a nerve passes over it. It's the funnybone, and when it's knocked it hurts a lot. Not funny!

What were the Snake Charmer's last words? "Don't worry, he's ARMLESS!

Ouch...now that hurts!

5

Strong or bung

Did you know bone is stronger than concrete? It's
true! In fact, bone is 40 times as strong. Have you seen
kung-fu or karate kings break slabs of concrete with
one bare hand?

Whack!!!
They
are
specially
trained to
do it without
busting their own bones –
so please don't try it yourself.

What makes bones so strong?

There are two types of bone tissue. The outer layer of a bone is very hard and is made of **compact** bone tissue. It's thickest in our limbs and especially our legs, giving us strength for walking and weight-bearing. **Cancellous** bone tissue looks like a sponge or honeycomb, and is hard and light. It's found at the end of long bones and in short bones. In flat bones, cancellous bone is like the filling of a sandwich between two layers of compact bone.

The structure of the 'honeycomb' in cancellous bone gives bone its great strength. It can withstand forces from different directions.

A tough membrane, the periosteum, covers all bones. It's full of blood vessels bringing nutrients into the bone through lots of tiny canals.

MARVELLOUS MARROW

The honeycomb 'holes' of cancellous bone are filled with soft, squishy marrow. It can be red or yellow.

Red bone marrow produces **blood** cells. Babies are

born with only red marrow in their bones, but from about the age of five onwards, some of it starts becoming yellow and fatty, and no longer produces blood cells.

LIFESAVERS

Lots of people between 18 and 50 can become lifesavers without any training at all. How? They donate some of their bone marrow to a person who's in danger of dying soon. It can be the gift of life.

Bone marrow contains stem cells, the cells that in turn produce blood cells.[2] Sometimes bone marrow doesn't work properly, or the blood cells it does produce are destroyed by a disease or chemotherapy. Bone marrow transplanted from someone else will often produce healthy, new blood cells that give a sick person a chance to recover. It's a treatment that's used for a number of illnesses, including leukaemia.

The marrow can be donated by an identical twin,

[2] Stem cells can develop into all sorts of different cells, apart from blood. They are also found in the umbilical cord of newborn babies.

or by another relative, or by a stranger whose bone marrow matches the patient's. Sometimes there's only one known person who can save the life of a child or adult on the other side of the world. Bone marrow can also be taken from the patient (at the hip) when they are well and given back to them later, through a tube, when they're sick. In two to three weeks, healthy blood cells start appearing again.

TOO TALL OR TOO SHORT

A hormone produced in the pituitary gland at the base of the brain makes us grow. Boys and girls who produce too much of this hormone, before the cartilage in their long bones has ossified, grow too tall – sometimes close to 3 metres. Their condition is called gigantism.

Adults who produce too much of the hormone develop thickened bones and also grow very tall. Their condition is called acromegaly. To reduce the amount of growth hormone, doctors can operate on the pituitary gland, or give radiotherapy or medicines.

If the pituitary gland doesn't produce *enough* growth hormone, boys and girls will be extremely short. Sometimes they are treated with a synthetic growth hormone to help them grow taller.

Lots of countries have associations for very short people. They refer to themselves as short-statured, or 'Little People', or as having restricted growth. It's very offensive to call them midgets.

FAULTY FUSIONS

In the roof of your mouth is the upper palate – two bones that fused before birth. You can feel the fusion line with your tongue. If these bones don't join properly before a baby is born, it will have a gap there – a **cleft palate**. If the palate doesn't fuse below the nose, the gap there is called a **cleft lip**. (It used to be known as a hare lip because it looked like the upper lip of a hare.) Nobody knows why the palate bones don't fuse. It happens in about 1 in 600 babies.

Babies with both a cleft palate and a cleft lip often have difficulty feeding and may need special aids to help sucking and swallowing. Later they may need the help of a speech pathologist too. Luckily the clefts can be repaired with bone grafts.

Occasionally a baby is born with part of the spinal cord poking out of its back: it has **spina bifida**. Why? Some of the vertebrae that should protect the cord didn't grow properly in the first weeks of pregnancy. The baby is at great risk of infection until the back is closed by surgeons and antibiotics are given. If the spinal cord has been damaged, babies with spina bifida will suffer some paralysis in their lower body.[3]

DOING THE CALCIUM CRUNCH!

Most of the body's calcium is stored in our bones. What for?

Besides keeping our bones and teeth strong, calcium is drawn out for use in muscles and nerves. It keeps our heartbeat steady, and it helps our blood clot when we cut ourselves (so blood doesn't pour out all over the place).

One of the best sources of calcium is . . . bones. Dogs, including foxes, wolves and jackals, gnaw them, bury them and gnaw them again, dirt and all.

Saltwater crocodiles are bone-crushers. Snap! If you're extremely lucky you might escape with a broken arm or leg. But it's more likely the croc will go into a death roll and you'll drown in its jaws. Crocodiles gulp

[3] The good news is that if women take folic acid (Vitamin B9) before and during the early weeks of pregnancy, the risk of having a baby with spina bifida is much less.

the bones of their prey, as well as the flesh, the fur and the feathers. They don't chew food the way we do, so a powerful acid in their stomach breaks down the bones for digestion.

Pythons that swallow mice and rats also digest their prey's bones, although not the fur – that comes out in the droppings.

Cuttlebone that pet birds eat is not bone, although it does contain calcium. It's the internal shell of the invertebrate cuttlefish – a member of the squid family.

People eat bones, too. Salmon and sardine bones soften during the canning process, which makes them edible. In Asia a small fish called silver or sand whiting grows to about the length of a ruler. Its backbone can be deep-fried and eaten as a 'nibble'.

SAVED BY SUNSHINE AND SPINACH

If crunching bones makes you shudder, you'll find calcium in dairy foods such as milk, yoghurt, butter and cheese. Leafy green vegetables, almonds and baked beans also contain it. But there's a catch. To absorb calcium properly, we need Vitamin D. Luckily our bodies are able to make Vitamin D when our skin is exposed to sunlight. If you walk to and from school you'll get enough through your face and hands.

What if you don't walk to school and you wouldn't drink a sardine and spinach milkshake in a fit? Western diets are so rich that most of us get more than enough of everything. But in poorer countries children *don't* always get enough calcium or Vitamin D. They can suffer from rickets: their bones will be soft and bent.

OSTEO-WHAT?

Some old people have very fragile bones that break easily. They have osteoporosis (ostee-o-por-*oh*sis). If it's bad, they don't even have to fall to get a fracture – a cough or a sneeze can be enough.

From about the age of 35 onwards, everyone starts to lose more calcium and other minerals from bone than their bodies can replace. This is 'bone loss'. *Severe* bone loss is osteoporosis. Old women *and* men shrink because of it.

MASS MOVEMENT

Can you avoid osteoporosis? Maybe you can. For a start, you can build bone mass through exercise – weight-bearing exercise, that is.

Lift your own weight by walking and climbing, doing chin-ups and push-ups. You hate sport? Apart from walking to school, you can walk to the shops or the park or round the block with the dog. Climb stairs instead of using the lift, try trampolining or take up tap-dancing. Encourage the oldies in your family to walk and exercise, too.

Weight-lifters have great bones as well as hard-to-believe muscle. Shearers and bricklayers who do heavy physical work have more bone mass than people who sit at a desk all day and in front of TV all night.

Too many Computer games

LOST IN SPACE

Astronauts lose a lot of bone mass in space. Because of this, manned space flights to Mars can't happen yet. The lack of gravity – weightlessness – means astronauts float through their spacecraft instead of walking, so they aren't bearing their own weight.

Scientists are developing special exercise equipment to prevent astronauts' bone loss. They already know that standing on a lightly vibrating board helps. This research will also help people on earth who suffer from osteoporosis, as well as boys and girls with cerebral palsy who are unable to walk and exercise.

SHOOK-UP SHEEP

Scientists have done an experiment giving 20-minute doses of vibration to sheep's hind legs. After a year the bones of these animals had grown faster and stronger than the bones of ordinary sheep. It's true! And guess what made them think of it? Somehow someone found out that cats purred at just the right frequency for bone growth. That's the frequency used on the sheep.

6

Weaver's bottom and housemaid's knee

Have you ever sprained your wrist or twisted your ankle? Do you know someone who suffers from tennis elbow? Does your grandfather grumble about gout, or Aunt Bertha bark, 'Mind my bunion!' if you step on her big toe? All these are problems of **joints**, places where two bones meet.

Q. What holds our bones to other bones, so we don't collapse like a bundle of pick-up-sticks?

A. Tough bands of fibre called **ligaments**.

Q. What holds muscles to bones?

A. Tough bands of fibre called **tendons**.

Joints, ligaments, muscles and tendons allow us to sit, stand or squat, shrug our shoulders, turn cartwheels, hold a pen, kick a football, chew food, dance, turn on a tap, pick flowers, hug someone, climb a tree, sew, write, use scissors, slap a mozzie, stroke the cat . . . and so on.

We have three types of joints in our bodies.

Fibrous joints, where bones – such as the ones in your skull – are held together so tightly almost no movement is possible.

Cartilaginous joints, such as the discs of cartilage that are flexible and act as shock absorbers between the vertebrae of your spine.

Synovial joints, which have a cartilage lining and contain small amounts of synovial fluid. This fluid lubricates the joint structures, just as machinery oil lubricates engines. There are six types of synovial joints that let our bodies move in all sorts of ways.

» **Ball and socket joints**, such as our *hips* and *shoulders*. The ball end of one bone fits into the socket of another and lets the bones rotate in various directions. The *shoulder* is the most mobile joint in our body.

» **Condyloid joints** are similar, but flatter than ball and socket joints. This means less circular motion is possible. Your *knee* is a condyloid joint.

» **Pivot joints**, such as the *first two cervical vertebrae of the neck*, have a peg of one bone fitting into the ring of another so that a simple rotation, or swivelling, can occur – like shaking your head for 'No!'

>> **Hinge joints**, like a door, allow movement forwards and backwards on the one plane. The rounded surface of one bone fits over the rounded surface of the bone it meets. This is how *elbows* work.

>> **Saddle joints** have surfaces like a saddle that allow a combination of movements. Wriggle your *thumbs* about and see how they move differently from your fingers.

>> **Gliding joints** are where the flat surfaces of two bones glide against each other. This happens with the carpals when you bend your *wrists*, and the tarsals in your *feet* when you walk.

A LO-O-ONGER NIGHT

When you get up in the morning you are slightly taller than at bedtime. Why? Standing and sitting during the day puts pressure on the discs of cartilage between the vertebrae, which makes them flatten slightly. Lying down takes the pressure off, so they swell a tiny bit. Try measuring yourself.

NO-JOKE JOINTS

Joints can be a source of pain. When you have **gout**, needle-sharp chemical crystals form in the joints – often a joint in the big toe. Walking becomes agony, and some people go barefoot when they have an attack because they can't bear wearing shoes.

Arthritis means inflammation of the joints, and it always hurts. In **osteo-arthritis** the cartilage lining of the joint is damaged. In **rheumatoid arthritis** the synovium that produces the synovial fluid has become inflamed. Boys and girls can suffer from a troublesome type called **juvenile rheumatoid arthritis**.

Orthopaedic surgeons operate on people to replace and reconstruct the bones of damaged hips and knees with artificial ones made of metal and plastic.

GRRRRRR

In traditional Chinese medicine, powdered tiger bones were used for hundreds of years to relieve arthritis. Now tigers are protected.

A PAIN IN THE ... AND OTHER PLACES

Some joints have a small sac of fluid called a bursa. Inflammation of the bursa caused by infection or injury is called bursitis (ber-*sy*-tis). 'Weaver's bottom' is a condition that weavers used to suffer through sitting for years on hard stools as they worked. It's inflammation of the bursa of the ischium, a bone in your bottom.

'Housemaid's knee' is inflammation of a bursa on

the front of the kneecap, although you don't have to be a housemaid to get it. It can happen to anyone who kneels a lot, scrubbing or gardening or carpet-laying, because kneeling puts pressure on the knee joints.

BUNIONS MAKE YOU CRY LIKE ONIONS

Ever tried crossing your toes?

People who have worn pinching, pointed shoes for years may notice their big toe moving sideways towards the second toe and eventually crossing over it. The bursa in the big toe swells and hurts. That's what we call a bunion.

SPRAIN PAIN

When the ligaments of a joint stretch or tear, it's a sprain. If they are torn, they may need to be repaired by a surgeon.

Football players often suffer injuries to the knee such as strained ligaments, or a torn cartilage, which can mean hospital and months off the field.

An all-round sportsman

DISLOCATED AND DISAPPOINTED

When a footballer is taken off with a dislocated shoulder, what's happened? The head of the humerus (upper arm bone) has come out of its socket in the scapula – the shoulder blade. Ligaments and tendons may be torn at the same time. Ouch!

TENDON TRAUMA

Bang! Whack! Bang! Whack! Repeated movements in tennis can damage an elbow tendon, and the painful result is then diagnosed as tennis elbow.

Golfers sometimes damage a different tendon in their elbow, and that's called (surprise) golfer's elbow.

60

7

X and ‡

If you've crashed off a trampoline or fallen downstairs or been in a car accident, you'll feel the pain, you'll see the swelling, bruising or blood, and you might yell. But what will show if you've broken a bone?

MYSTERY RAYS

German physicist Wilhelm Conrad Röntgen was working with light and electrical current in his laboratory in 1895. Imagine how amazed he must have been to see the bones *inside* his hand displayed on a screen. He named the rays 'X' because he didn't know what type of radiation they were. In Germany they are called after him: *Röntgenstrahlen*.

X-ray pictures caused huge excitement. Just as photographers took photographs of families and individuals, people set up studios to take pictures of people's bones – radiographs. A few people worried about what might be seen through their clothes! Doctors quickly realised how useful radiology would be for diagnosis, and by 1896 hospitals were installing X-ray equipment.

Then scary things started to happen. The hair of X-ray photographers' (radiographers') hands fell out. Blisters and burns appeared on their skin. Some years later an assistant in an X-ray manufacturing laboratory died. A few radiographers took simple precautions such as reducing the amount of time they and patients were exposed to the rays, but people continued to die from the effects of radiation. Nevertheless, the value of X-rays to medicine was clear and in 1901 Röntgen was awarded the Nobel Prize for physics.

A monument in Hamburg, Germany, names over 300 people from different countries who died in the process of developing radiology.

BLOCKOUT AND BADGES

Radiographers X-ray people all day and every day,
so they have a greater risk of absorbing a dangerous
amount of radiation than patients. In an X-ray room
the radiographer puts the patient in position, then
walks behind a safety screen to take the pictures.
The screen is impregnated with lead (or equivalent)
to block scattered radiation that might enter the
radiographer's body. But they will absorb some, so they
wear a film badge to measure how much. The badges
are checked regularly to ensure the radiation level
hasn't gone above a certain amount.

In an operating theatre, radiographers wear a lead (or lead-equivalent) rubber apron for protection, as well as a badge to measure radiation. Radiologists and some surgeons wear a ring with a chip, a bit like a diamond ring. The rings, like badges, measure how much radiation has been absorbed when the doctor's fingers are close to the part of the patient's body that's being X-rayed. If fingers are repeatedly exposed to radiation over a long time, a malignant tumour may develop and that could mean the end of a surgeon's career.

CAT WITH NO MIAOW

A CAT scanner – **c**omputerised **a**xial **t**omography – uses X-rays to produce digital pictures of bones. They show three dimensions (depth, length and breadth), or through-the-body thin slices on a computer. These cross-sections can, for example, reveal facial fractures that may not show clearly on an ordinary X-ray because some facial bones overlap each other.

(For soft tissue such as ligaments and muscles, an MRI scanner – **m**agnetic **r**esonance **i**maging – is used.

It scans the body using powerful magnetism and soundwaves instead of radiation. It can be taken in any plane – vertical, oblique or horizontal – and can reveal body parts not seen in CAT scans.)

REPAIR KIT

Doctors' shorthand for a bone fracture (break) is #, the same as the symbol for a sharp in music. But it's nothing to sing about when it happens. It hurts!

Luckily, bone mends itself with bone when it's been broken. Other parts of the body repair themselves with fibrous tissue that leaves a scar. Teeth, the brain and the spinal cord can't mend themselves at all.

A fractured rib is painful, but it can mend itself. Other broken bones need to be held still so they will

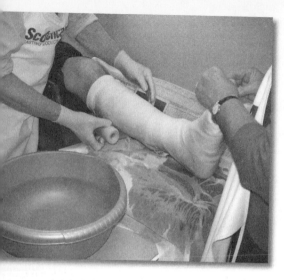

mend in the correct position. For a broken finger a **splint** (something rigid) is sometimes enough. The plaster **cast** that you'd have for a bigger bone in an arm or a leg does the same thing. It holds the two parts of the bone in line and completely still so they mend straight. If they mend crookedly you might end up with a limp, or stiff joints that cause problems with certain movements.

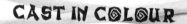

CAST IN COLOUR

Casts are now often made of fibreglass.
It's lighter than plaster and doesn't go out of shape
if it gets wet. And it comes in various colours!
The idea may have come from surfies who use
fibreglass to mend their boards.

For a bad break, an orthopaedic surgeon (a surgeon who specialises in mending bones) may insert stainless steel or titanium screws to hold the pieces of bone together. If bone has been lost, bone from another part of the patient's body may be grafted on.

The bad news is that your sporting career is over... but the good news is you have a great future in the movies

Children's bones are softer than adult ones because they haven't completely ossified, so sometimes they bend without breaking, or they don't break all the way through. This is a **greenstick fracture**.

In **open fractures**, the break is exposed to air through torn skin. There's a risk of infection to the bone, so the doctor will prescribe antibiotics, put the bone back together, and stitch up the skin.

8

Suspect, studied, stolen

In 1911 Charles Dawson, a solicitor and amateur geologist, discovered a skull and bone fragments at the village of Piltdown in Sussex, England. Scientists were very excited. They thought the bits of bone were human fossils 500 000 years old. Were these the 'missing link' between apes and humans?

Forty years later the scientists found they'd been fooled. The fossils were fakes. The 'skull' was actually a human cranium (brainbox) plus an orang-utan jawbone. Some of the bone pieces had been stained dark brown to make them appear fossilised, but radiocarbon dating showed them to be less than 1000 years old.

By the time the hoax was exposed, Charles Dawson was dead. But was he the culprit? And if so, had he acted alone?

As well as Dawson, the list of suspects includes respected scientists of the day, a priest, a librarian, a jeweller and even Sir Arthur Conan Doyle, the author of the famous Sherlock Holmes  detective stories. But since they are now in their graves too, the true story of the Piltdown find remains a mystery.

Piltdown Man was a hoax, but palaeontologists have since found real human fossils, and pre-human ones as well.

BECOMING A FOSSIL

Fossil bones are formed when a creature dies in a watery area and is buried quickly by sand or mud. Water containing minerals seeps into the bones. Over thousands of years the bones mineralise or petrify and become a hard copy of the original ones.

CRANIUM BRAINIUM

One of the ways the different types of humans and human ancestors can be told apart is through the size of their cranium (the round part of a skull).

Your brain sits inside your cranium and is protected by it. Like petrol motors, cranium sizes are measured in cubic centimetres. The average for a modern adult is around 1450 cubic centimetres – the size of a small car engine. A baby's cranium is around 395 cubic centimetres – the engine capacity of a lawn-mower.

LITTLE OLD LUCY

Australopithecus was a pre-human genus whose fossilised bones were first found in Southern Africa. *Pithecoid* means ape-like and *australis* means southern. The four species of *Australopithecus* lived from 4 million to 1 million years ago. They walked on two feet and had a cranium size of 450 to 600 cubic centimetres.

'Lucy' is an *Australopithecus afarensis*. Donald Johanson found Lucy's fossilised bones in Ethiopia, northern Africa, in 1974. These are seriously old bones. Lucy lived about 3.2 million years ago! She was tiny – just over a metre tall. But Johanson could tell she was fully grown because her wisdom teeth had come through and were worn down from years of use. Her bones showed signs of arthritis too. They're now in the Addis Ababa Museum in Ethiopia.

HANDY HUMANS

Homo habilis (Latin for handy man – of course there were handy women too) lived in East Africa around

2 million years ago. They were the *first* human beings. At 750 cubic centimetres, their brain space was larger than that of the *Australopithecines*. They were able to make tools. For instance, *Homo habilis* sharpened stones for cutting meat, instead of using sticks and rocks they'd just picked up.

Homo erectus, which means 'upright man', lived between 1.8 million and 250 000 years ago. This species of human had a bigger brain than *Homo habilis*. Members of *Homo erectus* used fire, which meant they could cook food. And they began to move out of Africa. One of the best-known fossils of *Homo erectus* is Java Man. His bones were discovered on the island of Java in Indonesia in 1891.

Homo sapiens, 'wise man' or 'thinking man', evolved around 195 000 years ago. The skull had enlarged to 1450 cubic centimetre capacity. *Homo sapiens* spread throughout the world, hunted with arrows, and drew pictures on cave walls. This is the group **modern** humans evolved from more than 90 000 years ago.

Cro Magnons lived 30 000 to 40 000 years ago. They were a form of *Homo sapiens*, and their fossils were found in France in 1868. But Cro Magnons are extinct and we are still here: the only surviving species of the genus *Homo*.

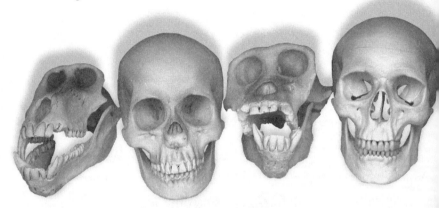

MYSTERY MAN

Fossilised bones of a different human species were first found in the Neander Valley in Germany in the 1800s. This species was called Neanderthal (nee-ander-tahl) Man, and since then more of their bones have been found in other European countries and the Middle East. Neanderthals lived from around 200 000 to 30 000 years ago. They were heavier-boned than modern humans, and they had bigger brains – about 1600 cubic centimetres. How closely were they related to us?

Did they breed with our *Homo sapiens* ancestors? And who killed them off – the Cro Magnons? Scientists are still working on the answers.

MINI HUMANS

In 2004 scientists announced their discovery of fossils and bones of a previously unknown species of human, *Homo floriensis*, on the island of Flores in Indonesia. They were nicknamed 'hobbits' because of the small size of their skeletons. As adults, these people were only a metre tall. They're now extinct, but it seems village legends about hairy little people who once lived on Flores may be true.

WANT A DATE?

Palaeo-anthropologists use radiocarbon dating to estimate the age of bones up to 50 000 years old. All living creatures contain carbon, which lessens steadily after death. The quantity of a certain kind of carbon left tells scientists how long ago the bone was alive.

Uranium tests and potassium-argon dating are other methods scientists use to find out how old fossils are.

WANTED: OLD BONES FOR HOME

Archaeologists, explorers, missionaries, private collectors and others have dug up or found human bones and sent them to museums around the world. For a long time Australian Aborigines, New Zealand Maoris, Native Americans and Peruvians have pleaded for the return of bones of their forebears. Sometimes museums don't want to give them back because scientists are studying them. In 2006 the Natural History Museum of London agreed to return the remains of 17 Tasmanian Aborigines. The Smithsonian Institute in the USA is returning remains of Native Americans.

NICKED!

Santa Claus – Saint Nicholas – was born in Turkey in the third century and became the Bishop of Myra (now called Demre). He was buried in the church there, but a thousand years ago Italian pirates are said to have stolen his bones. They took them to a crypt beneath a church in Bari, Italy. Now Turkey wants the bones back. But Santa Claus's resting place attracts tourists, so Bari doesn't want to give up the bones.

The True Meaning of Xmas

9

Made from bone

How did people live thousands of years ago? They didn't take photographs, and rock paintings don't tell us much. What clues *did* they leave? Bones.

DIG THAT!

Often, but not always, bones are excavated from deep in the ground, which is why an archaeological site is called a 'dig'. In the 1980s a dig in Greenland revealed how people there lived more than 4000 years ago. They hunted seals using harpoons tipped with antler – and tossed aside the seal bones after eating the flesh. Their tools were made from bone and antler.

Stone-Age flutes made from the wing bones of cranes were discovered in China at a dig. They are 7000 to 9000 years old.

An early form of Chinese writing appears on oracle bones of the Shang Dynasty, 1700 to 1100 BCE. Often the marks were carved onto the shoulder blades of oxen (cattle), so it's sometimes called bone script. Questions about the weather or health or fortune were asked, and the bones – the oracles – were then heated so that cracks appeared. The cracks were interpreted and the results then carved onto the bone.

SEWN WITH BONE AND DRESSED TO IMPRESS

Excavated needles, buttons, necklaces and combs all made of bone show us the skills ancient people possessed.

Bones are still worn for decoration. How about a bone through the nose?

Some people in Papua New Guinea insert a bone from a flying fox there when they're in full ceremonial dress.

Sculptor Linde Ivimey takes bones home from restaurants for her works of art. She created 'The Little Emperor': a child in a highchair with fingers of bone, dressed in a bodysuit of turkey and chicken bones, and wearing a bone crown.

CORSET'S NOT BONE

In the 1800s lots of women were squashed and laced into corsets that were kept stiff with rods of whalebone.

Whalebone isn't bone. It's baleen, a flexible, horny substance that some whales have in their mouths to strain their food from the seawater – until they're harpooned. Then their baleen is sold as whalebone.

SOUP SLURP

In Australian abattoirs the long bones from sheep and cattle are cut up for export to Asian countries. Bones are an essential ingredient of soups that are popular there. Beef rib-cage bones are exported for spare-rib dishes as well as soups. Other bones are put through crushing machines and end up as a powder-like ingredient in flavouring sachets for instant noodles.

Leftover bones from cooked chicken, lamb and beef dishes can be boiled up on the kitchen stove to make stock – a broth that's used in soups.

GOING BANANAS FOR A FEED

Lots of bones and meat and fat from abattoirs go to rendering plants (factories). There they're cooked together at high pressure to produce meatmeal and a fatty substance called tallow.

Meatmeal is heavy and crumbly and contains fine bone chips. It's high in protein and is an ingredient in pellet food for fish and chickens.

Blood and bone is a fertiliser made from meatmeal and other products. It's sealed in plastic bags that keep most of the smell in, but once it's sprinkled on the garden . . . poooooooooooooh! Your dog will go bananas and might even try to eat it. The plants will guzzle it to give you great flowers and vegetables.

Tallow looks like liquid butter when it comes out of the abbattoir's pressure cooker. It's mixed into high-grade pellets to feed cattle and pigs, and is also used to make soap and candles.

BEST CHINA

Lift up a white china plate to the light, and hold your other hand behind it. If you can see your hand's shadow, the plate is probably *bone* china – and your mother will say, 'Hey, watch it! That's precious!'

Bone china is made from the ash of animal bones mixed with pure kaolin (china clay) and stone. Although it looks delicate, it's very hard and doesn't chip easily. Josiah Spode developed his formula for bone china in England over 200 years ago. Spode china is still produced and prized today.

OUT OF A SHEEP'S ANKLE

Have you ever played Fivestones or Jacks or Jackstones or Dibs? They're all the same game: knucklebones. In prehistoric times people played it in caves and later so did ancient Romans and Greeks.

Then, knucklebones came from the 'ankle' joints of sheep or goats, but these days they're usually plastic imitations.

GET SET

Every time you eat a marshmallow, gulp down a capsule, lick an ice-cream or chew a fruit gum, you're probably swallowing something made with boiled bones. True. All these have gelatine in them.

Gelatine is a protein made from boiled-up animal bones, skin, tendons and ligaments, and yet it's almost tasteless. It's sold in leaf, powder and granule form. Have a look in your kitchen – you might find a packet of gelatine on a shelf. It's in jelly crystals, too.

Gelatine binds foods together to give them a jelly-like consistency. Or it can make other foods, such as certain yoghurts, light and creamy. The pharmaceutical industry uses gelatine to make capsules that can be filled with medicines. Camera light filters and photographic film contain gelatine. Even playing cards and some smooth types of paper are coated with it. Gelatine is everywhere!

You know reading that makes my legs feel like jelly

Yeah, and my head feels like a marshmallow!

BONESPEAK

Bones have gnawed their way into our language. For instance, 'to have a bone to pick with someone' means to want to complain to them about something. 'Bonfire', surprisingly, is another example. Long ago it was spelt 'bonefire' because it was a fire made of bones. The fat in the bones made the fire burn well.

Here are some other expressions – if you don't know these, you can look them up, and maybe string them together in a story.

A Bone to Pick!

a skeleton in the cupboard
numskull
an **old fossil**
a **boneshaker**
a **skeleton key**
to **make old bones**
to **bone up on**
close to the bone
to **feel something in your bones**
lazybones
chilled to the bone
dry as a bone
bone idle
to **rap someone over the knuckles**
to **make no bones about something**
bare bones

DIANA LAWRENSON spreads blood and bone on her garden, drinks occasionally from bone-china cups, and stirs home-made soup at her stove while her skeleton keeps her upright. She has a bone in her nose but not through it, and is thankful her feet show no sign of a bunion. The phalanges in her fingers have tapped out books about ballet, guide dogs, pigs, chooks, hair, and now bones. She's currently working on a story about bone-gulping crocodiles.

GEOFF KELLY has been drawing funny pictures for a very long time. Until this book he'd concentrated on drawing the outside of people, but now he realises that the inside is more fun. He'd like to illustrate other similar books – maybe something like 'You can lassoo cattle with your intestines'?

THANKS

I had little more than a skeleton knowledge of bones when I knuckled down to write this book. My grateful thanks to the following people who kindly provided their expertise: orthopaedic surgeon Dr Harry Crock, molecular biologist Dr Bentley Atchison and forensic toxicologist Dr Jim Gerostamoulos of the Victorian Institute of Forensic Medicine, haematologist-oncologist Dr Karin Tiedemann of the Bone Marrow Transplant Program, Royal Children's Hospital, Victoria, Dr John Long of Museum Victoria, physiotherapist Jane Hellard, radiographer Christine Russell, Jonathan Ralph of Ralph's Meat Company, staff of the Underwater Zoo Melbourne Aquarium, Scott Pullyblank of Zoos Victoria, and Ann Spataro and staff of McLaughlin's Consolidated Fishermen Pty Ltd.

My thanks also go to editor Sarah Brenan with whom many facts were discussed, given humorous twists, poured in, debated, squeezed out, and finally . . . moulded into this little book.

As always, John gave me a great deal of support. This time, though, he broke his ankle. At last I was able to see first-hand a fibreglass cast being wrapped on and sawn off.

Diana Lawrenson

The publishers would like to thank istockphoto.com and the photographers named for images appearing on the following pages: i skeleton Kim Freitas, weights Kiyoshi Takahase Segundo; viii skeleton Marc Dietrich; 13 skull and crossbones, 22 vertebrae, 70 skull, various crossbones Nicholas Monu; 31 skeleton and 73 skulls Kenneth Zirkel. Thanks also for: page 7 facial reconstruction software from Wikipedia, © Jean N. Prudent; pages 19 (Rome Catacombs), 27 (moose antlers), 44 (giant) Library of Congress Prints and Photographs Division; page 28 Leonardo da Vinci drawing Geneva Foundation for Medical Education and Research website; pages 33 skull and 39 hand from *Gray's Anatomy*, 1918 edition; page 66 plaster cast the author; page 69 examining Piltdown remains, portrait painted by John Cooke in 1915; page 78 nose decoration Edward S. Curtis Collection, Library of Congress; pages 18 Sedlec Ossuary and 79 corset no attribution found.

WHERE TO FIND OUT MORE

Books for children

C. Ballard, *The Skeleton and Muscular System*, Wayland, England, 1997

Carol Ballard, *Bones: Injury, Illness and Health*, Heinemann, UK, 2003

D. Cordingly and J. Falconer, *Pirates Fact and Fiction*, Cross River Press, New York, 1992

Donna Jackson, *The Bone Detectives*, Little Brown & Co., USA, 1996

Norah Moloney, *The Young Oxford Book of Archaeology*, OUP, 1995

S. Parker, *Look at Your Body – Skeleton*, Aladdin Books, London, 1996

A. Royston, *Why Do Bones Break?*, Heinemann, Oxford, 2002

Websites

FORENSIC SCIENCE
- www.nifs.com.au
  At Education click on Fact Sheets and then on Skeletons

PARIS CATACOMBS
- www.ibiblio.org/wm/
  and click on Visit Paris, then Catacombs

FACIAL RECONSTRUCTION
- http://news.rgj.com/assets/html/J726701428.html

- http://news.nationalgeographic.com/news/2005/05/photogalleries/tut_mummy/

HUMAN ORIGINS
- www.mnh.si/anthro/humanorigins

BONE MARROW
- www.bmdi.org.au

X-RAYS
- www.howstuffworks.com

Books for teachers

R. McNeill Alexander, *Bones: the unity of form and function*, Weidenfeld and Nicholson, London, 1994

H.V. Crock, *An Atlas of Vascular Anatomy of the Skeleton and Spinal Cord*, Martin Dunitz, London, 1996

D.C. Johanson and A. Maitland, *Lucy, the Beginnings of Humankind*, Granada, London, 1981

H. Miller, *Secrets of the Dead*, Channel 4 Books, London, 2000

P. Thomas, *The Science of Forensic Anthropology*, Facts on File, New York, 1995

INDEX